Social and Emotional Learning Activities

GRADES 3–4

Writing: Guadalupe Lopez
Kathleen Jorgensen
Content Editing: Lisa Vitarisi Mathews
Teera Robinson
Copy Editing: Laurie Westrich
Art Direction: Yuki Meyer
Cover Design: Yuki Meyer
Illustration: Bryan Langdo
Design/Production: Jessica Onken

EMC 6097

Evan-Moor®

Visit
teaching-standards.com
to view a correlation
of this book.
This is a free service.

**Correlated to
Current Standards**

**Congratulations on your purchase of some of the
finest teaching materials in the world.**

*Photocopying the pages in this book
is permitted for single-classroom use only.
Making photocopies for additional classes
or schools is prohibited.*

For information about other Evan-Moor products, call 1-800-777-4362,
fax 1-800-777-4332, or visit our website, www.evan-moor.com.
Entire contents © 2021 Evan-Moor Corporation
18 Lower Ragsdale Drive, Monterey, CA 93940-5746. Printed in USA.

CPSIA: McNaughton & Gunn, Saline, MI USA [11/2022]

CONTENTS

I Am Happiest When...

Name: _____

Finish the sentences.

1. I am happiest when I am with _____.
tell who

2. I am happiest when I am _____.
tell where

3. I am happiest when I am _____.
tell what you're doing

Social and Emotional Learning Activities • EMC 6097 • © Evan-Moor Corp.

Do I Worry?

When people **worry**, they feel uneasy about something that could happen. Everyone worries sometimes, and worrying is normal. Try to remember that worrying about something means you care about it a lot.

Read each sentence. Then write a checkmark in the box to tell if you agree or disagree.

	Agree	Disagree
1. I worry that other people do not like me.	☐	☐
2. I worry that my culture is different from the cultures of my friends.	☐	☐
3. I worry that I am not smart enough.	☐	☐
4. I worry about my family.	☐	☐
5. I worry about my safety.	☐	☐

Write a paragraph to explain what you worry about and why.

6. _____

_____

_____

_____

When you feel **empathy**, you try to understand how someone else feels. You try to imagine what it's like to be that person. You can have empathy for anyone, even people you've never met or people you disagree with.

Read the story and the question. Then color the number of bars on the phone to show how much empathy you have for the character.

> 1 bar = You do not understand the character's feelings.
> 5 bars = You very much understand the character's feelings.

1. Shanice's dog Ruffles is missing. Shanice and her mom made a flier with Ruffles' picture, and they handed copies to all the neighbors. Shanice starts to cry when she thinks about Ruffles. She worries that he is cold and scared.

   How much empathy do you have for Shanice?

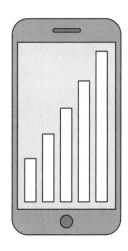

2. Ethan's best friend, Jake, borrowed a water bottle from Ethan. Jake didn't return the water bottle. So Ethan asked for it back after 2 weeks. Jake got mad and said, "Did you think I was going to steal it or something?" Jake finally returned the water bottle. But he and Ethan do not hang out with each other anymore, even though they used to be best friends.

   How much empathy do you have for Ethan?

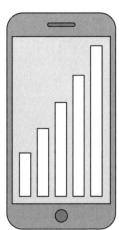

Social and Emotional Learning Activities • EMC 6097 • © Evan-Moor Corp.

Curiosity

You feel **curiosity** when you want to learn more about someone or something. Why is curiosity important? It has helped people survive for centuries by helping them learn about the world. And scientists believe that learning is good for people's health. What things are you curious about?

Finish the chart. First read the topic. Then write an **X** under **Yes** or **No** to tell if you are curious about this topic and want to learn more. Last, explain why you are or are not curious about the topic.

Topic	Yes	No	Why or why not?
How people from other countries live and what they do every day	😀	☹️	
How many different kinds of families there are and how they're like your family	😀	☹️	
Why every person is so different	😀	☹️	

Write any other topics you are curious about.

_____ _____

_____ _____

Marshmallow Word Cloud

Name: _____

Make a marshmallow word cloud using words that describe yourself!

What You Need

- paint or markers
- mini marshmallows
- glue
- colored construction paper

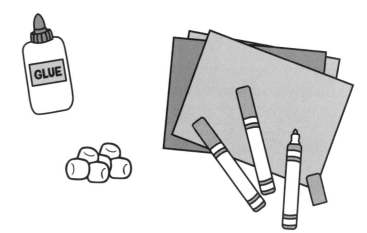

What You Do

1. Use paint or markers to color some of the marshmallows.

2. Make words out of mini marshmallows and glue the marshmallow words onto construction paper. Make words that tell about you. You can use any words and as many words as you want.

3. After you are finished making your word cloud, let it dry. Then share it with your friends and your family.

Social and Emotional Learning Activities • EMC 6097 • © Evan-Moor Corp.

Self-Management

Introduce self-management to your students.

Self-management is about making choices that you feel are helpful to you and to others. When you practice self-management, you think about how you want to treat others and yourself. You think about your behavior. And you think about things you want to do better. For example, some people want to be kinder to others. Some people want to get better grades in school. And some people want to be a better friend. Think about what kind of person you want to be. Think about what you want to do. Then think about what choices you can make to do that. You have the power to make good choices. As long as you are trying to be kind and respectful when you make a choice, you are doing great.

Topics covered in this unit:

Coping	Goals	Grit
Self-care	Responsibility	Self-kindness
Feedback	Mindfulness	

People Cope

The word **cope** means to deal with something that is difficult. People have different ways of coping with their feelings. Some ways of coping might be healthier than others. Think about the ways you choose to cope.

Imagine that you are very upset. Color the circle if the words inside tell something that could make you feel better. For the circles with no words, write something that you think could make you feel better.

Watching TV

Learning about a different culture from mine

Caring for a pet or seeing animals

Trying a food from a different country

Walking

Being outside

Taking a nap

Spending time with family

Texting

Playing video games

Eating my favorite foods

Listening to music

Sometimes we have a **goal**. This means we want to start doing something or get better at something. We can put effort into reaching our goals.

Clare wrote behavior goals for herself. She wrote them in a code because she doesn't want anyone else to know what her goals are. Use the key to uncover what Clare's goals are.

A	B	C	D	E	F	G	H	I	J	K	L	M
11	4	15	3	9	20	7	55	44	5	19	21	25

N	O	P	Q	R	S	T	U	V	W	X	Y	Z
32	1	12	8	17	6	18	2	14	23	67	99	26

Goal 1:

___ ___ ___   ___ ___
2   6   9   25   99

___ ___ ___ ___ ___ ___
44   32   3   1   1   17

___ ___ ___ ___ ___
14   1   44   15   9

Goal 2:

___ ___ ___   ___ ___ ___ ___ ___
6   44   18   6   18   44   21   21

___ ___ ___   ___ ___ ___ ___ ___ ___
11   32   3   21   44   6   18   9   32

I Have Grit

When we say a person has **grit**, we mean that person keeps trying something, even when it gets difficult. People with grit don't give up. Fictional characters in movies often have grit. Real people can have grit, too.

Think about a time when you had grit. What was difficult? How did you feel? Why did you keep trying?

Pretend someone made a movie about when you had grit. Draw an exciting poster for this movie. Write a title that will get people excited to see the movie.

Movie Title: _____

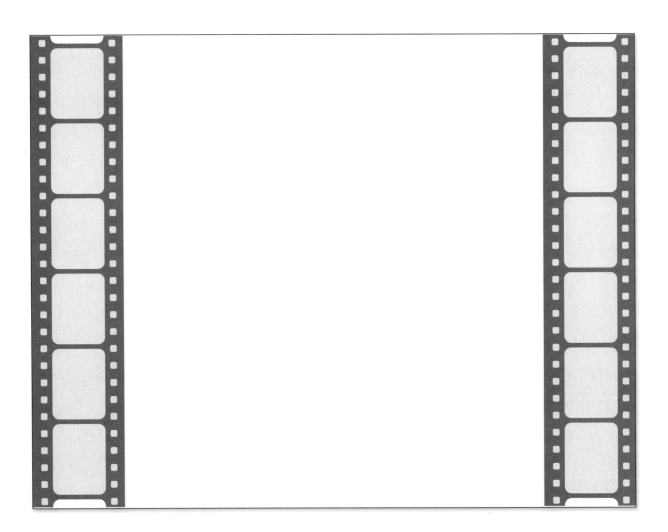

Responsibilities and Fun

Name: _____

Responsibilities, like brushing your teeth and going to school, are important. But having fun is important, too! Did you know that having fun is good for your health? Different things are fun for different people.

In the Venn diagram, write 3 things that you do for each category. You can also write things that you would like to start doing.

Responsibilities   **Both**   **Fun**

1.

2.

3.

Being Kind to Ourselves

It is important to take responsibility for our actions. But it is also important to forgive ourselves. Instead of blaming yourself for something, try to learn a lesson from what happened. And be kind to yourself. We all make mistakes!

Look at the kid and read the sentence. Then read the thought bubbles. Circle the thought that shows self-kindness.

1. Minhee did her homework, but she forgot to bring it to school.

Well, it's okay. I will try not to forget my homework again.

I can't do anything right!

2. During the concert, Tyreek played a wrong note on his violin.

I'm glad I practiced a lot. I only made one mistake the whole night!

I'm so bad at playing music. I should just quit!

Look at the kid and read the sentence. Then write a thought for the kid that shows self-kindness.

3. Roxy missed the shot during the basketball game, and her team lost.

Feedback Can Help Us

Name: _____

When someone tells us that we made a mistake or that we should try doing something differently, they are giving us **feedback**. It can be hard to listen to feedback sometimes. Just remember: feedback helps us learn how to do something better.

Read the story.

At the sound of the whistle, Marco ran as fast as he could. He wanted to win this race! He was already way ahead of the other runners. Soon, though, he felt his legs slow down. The other runners seemed to go faster. One by one, they passed Marco. The race ended with Marco in last place. "You started too fast, Marco," the P.E. teacher said. "You need to pace yourself. Then you won't get worn out so quickly." Marco already felt like he failed. The teacher's words made him feel even worse.

In the boxes below, write two different ways Marco could choose to react to the teacher's feedback. Then write what could happen after.

How Marco could react	What could happen after
1.	
2.	

Thinking About Our Actions

Name: _____

Read each action. Then write a ✓ to tell how often you think you do this action.

Actions	Never	Sometimes	A lot
Keeping your hands to yourself	☐	☐	☐
Really listening when someone else is speaking to you	☐	☐	☐
Looking at a person who is speaking to you	☐	☐	☐
Welcoming someone new	☐	☐	☐
Washing your hands, using a tissue, and doing other things to help protect yourself and others from germs	☐	☐	☐
Pointing at someone you are talking about	☐	☐	☐
Whispering or telling secrets in front of people who are not being told the secret	☐	☐	☐
Laughing at how someone looks, talks, or acts	☐	☐	☐
Staring at other people for a long time	☐	☐	☐
Saying something that isn't very nice without thinking about it first	☐	☐	☐
Rolling your eyes at someone after they say or do something	☐	☐	☐

Social and Emotional Learning Activities • EMC 6097 • © Evan-Moor Corp.

Coping Toolbox

Name: _____

It's okay to feel angry or unhappy sometimes. When you feel this way, it's important to pull out your "coping toolbox." Everyone has "coping tools." These are things that you know you like to do and that sometimes help you feel okay, or at least a little bit better.

Which coping tools from the list below might work for you? Choose four and write them on the lines below.

rip paper   talk about it

bounce a ball   write about your feelings

do exercise   draw a picture

squish clay   get some rest

1. _____

2. _____

3. _____

4. _____

Helpful or Harmful?

Name: _____

Everyone has different feelings at different times. Sometimes we feel fine. And sometimes we have feelings that don't feel so good. Having different feelings is okay.

The list below tells some things that people might choose to do when they feel upset. Read each item in the list. Then write it under **Helpful** or **Harmful**.

Yell at someone	Hit yourself
Break something	Eat a healthy snack
Take deep breaths	Listen to music
Talk to a friend	Hug someone
Kick someone	Get some rest

Helpful

_____

_____

_____

_____

_____

Harmful

_____

_____

_____

_____

_____

Social and Emotional Learning Activities • EMC 6097 • © Evan-Moor Corp.

Self-Care Clock

Self-care is anything that people do to take care of themselves so that they can feel healthy and well enough to do everything they want to do. Different people do different things for self-care.

On the clock, draw 3 things that you wish you could do more of during the day or that you wish you could start doing.

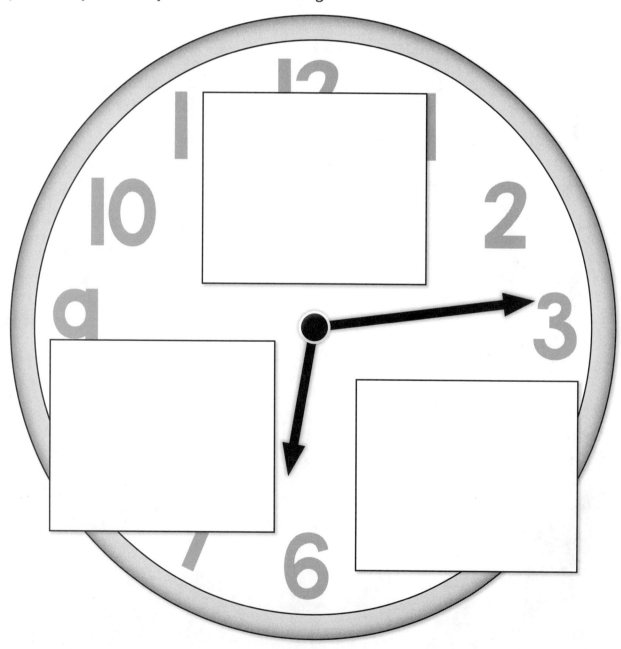

What Motivates You?

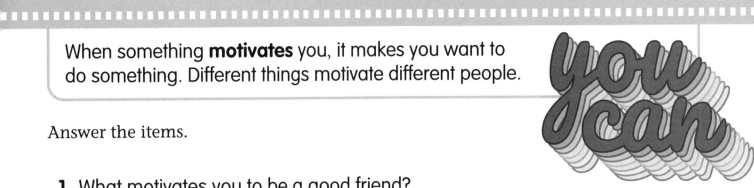

When something **motivates** you, it makes you want to do something. Different things motivate different people.

Answer the items.

1. What motivates you to be a good friend?

_____

_____

2. What motivates you to try hard in school?

_____

_____

3. What motivates you to make healthy choices?

_____

_____

4. Draw a picture that shows one thing you do to be a good friend.

Social Awareness

Introduce social awareness to your students.

When you have social awareness, you can sometimes tell how the people around you are feeling. People with social awareness care about other people's feelings and try to treat others with respect. We use social awareness when we stop ourselves from saying something that might hurt someone else's feelings. Social awareness helps you think about other people's opinions and points of view. Every person has a different view of the world because every person goes through different things in their lives. Social awareness helps us respect all people's opinions and feelings.

Topics covered in this unit:

Social cues   Empathy   Choices and consequences

Point of view   Emotions

Face and Body Talk

People use words to communicate by speaking, signing, and writing. But did you know that we also communicate without words? Our bodies and our faces can sometimes show how we are feeling or what we are thinking.

Look at the picture and answer the question.

1. Do you think the person in the picture looks confident? Explain your answer.

_____

_____

_____

_____

2. Imagine that you are talking to the person in the picture. Do you think that he seems like he is listening carefully to what you are saying? Explain your answer.

_____

_____

_____

_____

Have Empathy

Name: _____

When you understand how another person is feeling, you have **empathy** for that person. You might even feel the way that person feels. Empathy can help people get along with others.

Read the story. Think about how the character might feel. What would his or her face look like? What would the character do? On each face, draw the character and show his or her feelings.

Kids in school were talking about Jen behind her back. They made fun of her hair and clothes. They were even laughing at how she runs on the playground.

Enrique and his friends were racing on their bikes. He passed all of his friends, one by one. He felt lightning fast. Then he won! He had never gone faster than all of his friends before!

Feel Empathy

Name: _____

We do not know all of the hard things that other people have to go through. That is why it is important to try to be understanding of all people. When you try to understand how other people feel, you have **empathy**.

Read what each person said. Then color the circle to tell if the person's comment shows empathy.

1.

Look at Consuela's shoes. They are so old! I bet her parents don't love her enough to buy her new shoes that fit well.

○ empathy   ○ no empathy

2.

I asked Tyrone to come over after school, but he can't. He has to help take care of his mom every day. She has been sick for a long time. He helps make her food and clean the house. I wonder if sometimes he wishes he could just play with us after school instead of doing hard work.

○ empathy   ○ no empathy

3.

I can't believe that Melanie is picking on Oliver again! She laughs at him every day at recess. I bet he could use a friend.

○ empathy   ○ no empathy

Social and Emotional Learning Activities • EMC 6097 • © Evan-Moor Corp.

Choices Have Effects

The words inside the circle tell what a person could choose to do. The words inside the square tell what could happen as a result. Write inside the blank square to tell 1 other thing that could happen as a result.

1.

(calling your classmate a mean name)

Your teacher will let your parents know what you did.

2.

(making fun of students from other countries)

Later you will feel bad about making fun of them.

3.

(inviting everyone except 1 person from your class to your birthday party)

Your classmate will invite everyone but you to a party.

Everyone Sees Things Differently

Name: _____

Everyone sees things a little bit differently from everyone else. That's because all people have done and seen different things in their lives. We each think about things in our own way and have our own opinions.

Mel and his friends are talking. Read what each person says. Then answer the items.

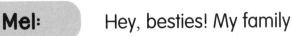

Mel: Hey, besties! My family adopted a dog this weekend! His name is Flint.

Firuz: Oh. Okay. I am surprised. I never knew that you wanted a dog. I thought you were like me. I don't really like pets.

Ryu: That's so awesome! I can't wait to meet your furry family member! I love the name your family chose!

Darius: Oh, that's not good! Now I don't know if I can ever come to your house again. I'll sneeze the entire time, I just know it!

Immy: Seriously? That is so weird. Why would you want a dog inside your house? Dogs are so messy.

Think about what each person said to Mel. How would you feel if you were Mel and you heard these responses? Write any emotions, or feeling words, next to each person's name below to tell how you would feel.

Firuz: _____

Ryu: _____

Darius: _____

Immy: _____

 Social and Emotional Learning Activities • EMC 6097 • © Evan-Moor Corp.

Everyone Sees Things Differently, continued

Name: _____

When you try to understand how someone else sees things, you have **empathy**. Empathy might help you understand why someone says and does certain things.

Read the stories about Immy and Ryu below. Then reread what they said to Mel on page 36. Think about how their stories might help to explain why they said what they said.

Immy just moved here from another country, where it is uncommon to have dogs for pets. In her country, animals are always kept outside.

Ryu's family has adopted 3 dogs, 2 cats, and a hamster from their local animal shelter. Everyone in Ryu's family loves pets.

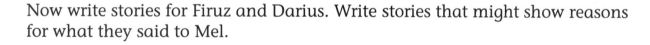

Now write stories for Firuz and Darius. Write stories that might show reasons for what they said to Mel.

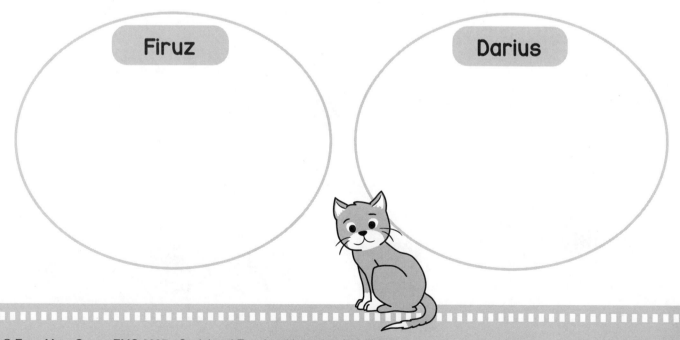

Firuz

Darius

Faces Show Feelings

Name: _____ EMC

Unscramble the emotion word in each cloud and write it on the line. Then draw the gingerbread person's face to match.

phapy

_____

asd

_____

rygan

_____

usidsrpre

_____

 Social and Emotional Learning Activities • EMC 6097 • © Evan-Moor Corp.

Social Cues

A smile might show that someone is happy. Crossed arms might show that a person does not feel friendly. These signals we make with our faces and bodies are called **social cues**. Social cues can sometimes help you understand how others are feeling.

The pictures below show people giving off social cues. The words in each box below show thoughts that match each social cue. Write the matching thought in each cloud.

Hi, I'm glad to see you!

I'm so tired.

I don't want to hear this.

Oops, I should not have said that!

1.

2.

3.

4.

Feelings and Greetings

Name: _____

Read the clue for each number below. Use the clue to help you unscramble the word. Write the word on the line.

Clue	Word to unscramble	
1. nobody to play with	yloeln	_____
2. run away and feel fear	dafria	_____
3. yawn and feel sleepy	rtied	_____
4. frown and cry	das	_____

Clue	Word to unscramble	
5. wave and greet	ohlel	_____
6. smile and laugh	ypaph	_____
7. cross your arms and stomp away	gryna	_____
8. jump and say "hooray!"	xecetid	_____

Feelings and Greetings,
continued

Name: _____

Write the words that you unscrambled in the crossword puzzle below. The numbers show where to write each word.

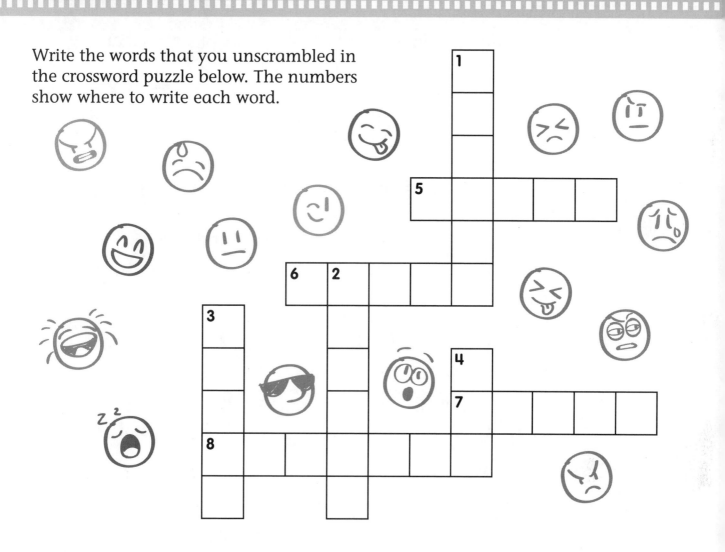

Now write your own clue for a feeling word. Then write the word next to the clue.

Clue   **Word**

_____   _____

_____

_____

Body Language

Saying that people use **body language** is another way of saying that people use their faces and bodies to communicate.

The words in the puzzle are about body language.
Find the words in the puzzle and circle them.

Find These Words:

EXPRESSION	SQUINT	LISTEN	SOCIAL	FROWN	QUIET
HANDS	VOICE	BODY	SMILE	WINK	LOUD

```
J  H  W  G  U  U  N  K  S  D  X  Q  N  B  G
I  X  A  W  Q  S  A  R  M  V  O  I  C  E  W
F  L  S  N  O  E  Q  Q  D  L  H  B  S  G  L
B  R  V  V  D  B  X  U  L  D  W  E  E  P  J
P  Z  P  R  U  S  C  P  I  I  D  D  L  N  Y
X  D  T  K  Q  I  Y  O  R  N  Z  F  O  W  F
L  I  S  T  E  N  L  O  M  E  T  Z  U  V  R
H  Y  D  P  L  R  T  N  W  E  S  A  D  J  O
P  T  W  B  S  Q  X  C  E  K  T  S  X  P  W
M  C  Z  Y  M  W  U  O  P  D  T  H  I  B  N
Y  E  B  E  I  N  T  I  A  I  P  Q  T  O  W
N  G  M  O  L  C  W  N  E  A  X  Q  C  D  N
H  N  U  O  E  K  I  B  F  T  I  L  R  Y  S
A  V  N  L  U  I  N  P  J  S  O  C  I  A  L
R  Y  N  Y  G  J  K  Q  S  T  Z  C  C  V  Q
```

Social and Emotional Learning Activities • EMC 6097 •

Responsible Decision-Making

Introduce responsible decision-making to your students.

You have the power to make choices, or decisions. When you do responsible decision-making, you try to make choices that are constructive, or helpful. You think about the results of your choices. You think about other people's feelings and how your choices will affect other people. You also think about how your choices will affect you later on. Think about the choices you make every day. You probably make some choices for your health. You probably make some choices for your safety. And you probably make a lot of choices because of how you feel. It is okay to use your feelings to help guide your choices. Try to also think about the feelings of others and what could happen after you make a choice.

Topics covered in this unit:

Responsibility	Choices and consequences	Accountability
Habits	Creating options for yourself	Commitment
Awkwardness	Cultural acceptance	

Responsibility Survey

Name: _____

Answer each question with your opinion. Draw a circle around **yes**, **no**, or **maybe**, or write sentences to tell your opinion.

Responsibility Survey

Are you always responsible for your own actions? **yes** **no** **maybe**	What does it mean to be responsible for your own actions? _____ _____
Is there ever a time when it is okay to lie? **yes** **no** **maybe**	Does anyone deserve to be bullied? **yes** **no** **maybe**
If you know that someone feels left out, do you feel like it is your job to help and include them? **yes** **no** **maybe**	Are other people's feelings important to you? **yes** **no** **maybe**
If you are really, REALLY mad at someone, does that make it okay to be rude to that person? **yes** **no** **maybe**	Is there ever a time when it is okay to break safety rules? **yes** **no** **maybe**

If you promise to feed your neighbor's pet while your neighbor is on vacation, but then you don't really feel like doing it, do you still have to do it?

yes   **no**   **maybe**

Social and Emotional Learning Activities • EMC 6097 • © Evan-Moor Corp.

List the Possible Outcomes

Some people find it helpful to make a list when they have to make a choice. You can make a list of all your choices. Or you can make a list of things that could happen later as a result of the choice you make.

Read the problem and choices in the chart.
Circle the choice you would choose.

Problem: Gregory is not friends with his classmate Zane, but he sees Darpinder and Noah pick on Zane every day. Gregory is friends with Darpinder and Noah. Yesterday they grabbed Zane's hat at recess and wouldn't give it back. This morning they took Zane's lunch out of his backpack and threw it away when Zane wasn't looking. Gregory doesn't like it when his friends are mean to Zane.

Choice 1: Tell an adult.
Choice 2: Stand up to Darpinder and Noah and tell them to stop picking on Zane.
Choice 3: Do nothing.
Choice 4: Tell Zane to fight Darpinder and Noah.

Think about your choice above. Then write 2 possible outcomes, or things that can happen later as a result of your choice.

Outcome 1:

_____

_____

Outcome 2:

_____

_____

Responsible Choices

Name: _____ • EMC 6097 • Evan-Moor

Sometimes we make choices to try to be happy, healthy, and safe.

Circle the picture with the choice that you think is most responsible.
Write why you think so.

	Choice 1:	Choice 2:	Why?
1.			_____ _____ _____
2.			_____ _____ _____
3.			_____ _____ _____

Social and Emotional Learning Activities • EMC 6097 • © Evan-Moor Corp.

You Can Make Other Choices

Sometimes things don't work out the way we want them to. When this happens, think about other choices you might be able to make.

Imagine that your best friend chose someone else to play with on the playground. Instead of not playing at all, what can you do? Draw yourself doing three other things that you could choose.

1.

2.

3.

Who Did It?

The choices we make are important. They can affect what happens later. Sometimes it isn't easy to know what the right choice is.

Your mother wants to know who broke the vase. You remember that you did it. What should you say to your mom? Write it in the speech bubble.

Do you think it is okay to not tell the truth sometimes?

◯ yes   ◯ no

Tell why or why not.

_____

_____

_____

Good Choices

Think of how you want your friends to treat you. You want them to be caring, respectful, and helpful. This is how you should treat your friends, too.

Look at the picture. Write a sentence telling if it's a choice you agree with or not. Explain your reason.

1.

_____

_____

2.

_____

_____

3.

_____

_____

4.

_____

_____

Get in the Habit

A **habit** is something you do often. Sometimes you do it without even thinking about it. The more you do a habit, the easier it becomes.

Read the healthy habits in the circles. Color the ones that you do.

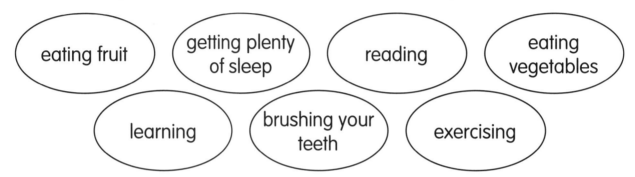

eating fruit

getting plenty of sleep

reading

eating vegetables

learning

brushing your teeth

exercising

Think about a healthy habit you do that is not named above. Write it in the arrow. Then draw a picture that shows you doing this habit in the box.

Read the habits that can be unhealthy. Color the ones you do sometimes.

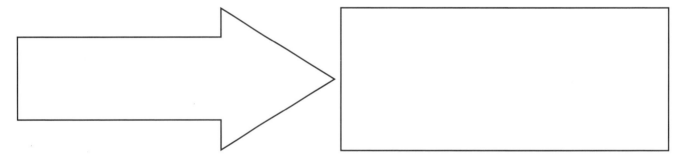

biting your nails

eating a large amount of candy

spending more time watching TV than doing any other activities

not washing your hands regularly

spending more time playing on a computer than doing any other activities

Make a Contract with Yourself

Name: _____

A **contract** is an agreement that is written or typed. It shows that a person agrees to do something.

Think about a new healthy habit that you want to start. Then finish the sentences below to create a contract.

CONTRACT

I, _____, hereby agree that from now on, I will
Write your name.

_____.
Describe your new habit or goal.

I will make sure to do this _____.
Write how often you will do this new habit.

I want to start this habit because _____

_____.
Write why you want to start this habit or why you have this goal.

Signature: _____

Date: _____

Make It Less Weird

Everybody gets into weird situations sometimes. Sometimes we feel weird because of something someone else said or did. And sometimes we feel like we said or did something weird.

Read about the situation that happened with Bashar and Tilda. Then answer the items.

On the class field trip, the teacher gave everyone a popsicle. Bashar and Tilda were talking while eating their popsicles. Bashar had a piece of popsicle in his mouth, and it fell out as he was talking. It landed on Tilda's shoe! It was so weird because nobody knew what to say. Tilda was quiet, and Bashar was quiet. They both just stared at the popsicle chunk on Tilda's shoe.

1. Write one thing that Bashar could do or say to make this situation less weird.

   _____

   _____

2. Write one thing that Tilda could do or say to make this situation less weird.

   _____

   _____

3. Write or draw a picture to tell about a time you were in a weird situation.

Weird Situations

Look at the pictures that show weird situations. Write an **X** in the circle under the picture if a situation like this has ever happened to you.

1.

2.

3.

4.

Welcoming Different Cultures into Your Life

Name: _____

Culture is part of how people live their lives. Many things are part of a culture, and lots of people celebrate more than one culture. One thing that helps give many people their culture is the country where they live.

Write 3 countries that have food and music you like. If you haven't eaten food or heard music from 3 different countries, then write the names of countries you think you would like food and music from. Read the examples.

Food			Music	
Germany	Pakistan		China	Mexico

Food

Music

Social and Emotional Learning Activities • EMC 6097 • © Evan-Moor Corp.

Relationship Skills

Introduce relationship skills to your students.

Relationship skills help us to have caring relationships with other people. We can practice habits that help us to communicate with others in a respectful way. We can also practice being understanding of others. Relationship skills help us tell other people that we disagree in a friendly way. They help us to be kind to the people we care about. The more we practice these skills, the better our relationships can be. These skills are all about having good conversations and relationships with others.

Topics covered in this unit:

Friendship	Respect	Tact
Conflict resolution	Listening skills	Coping
Communication	Constructive behavior	Social cues
Awkwardness	Cultural acceptance	Accountability

Friend Wanted!

Draw and write to finish the WANTED poster. Think about what makes a great friend and what you need in a friend.

WANTED

A _____ friend who is
adjective

_____ and _____.
adjective   **adjective**

Must like the things
shown in the pictures:

Must have these traits:

- Honest   ☐ yes   ☐ maybe   ☐ no
- Respectful   ☐ yes   ☐ maybe   ☐ no
- Fair   ☐ yes   ☐ maybe   ☐ no
- Loves animals ☐ yes   ☐ maybe   ☐ no
- Neat and tidy ☐ yes   ☐ maybe   ☐ no
- Funny   ☐ yes   ☐ maybe   ☐ no

A Better Way to Say It

Name: _____

Each box shows what Paola could say to her friend to get something she wants. Color the box that you think is a better way for Paola to communicate. Then explain why you chose the answer you did.

1.

If you don't help me with my homework, I'm gonna tell your mom that you lied, because you said you'd help me.

If you help me with my homework, I'll help you the next time you want help.

_____
_____
_____
_____

2.

Can you please ask your mom if we can do a sleepover at your house this weekend?

If you don't let me sleep over at your house this weekend, then you're never sleeping over at my house again.

_____
_____
_____
_____

3.

This is my house, and it's my video game, so I get to play longer than you.

I know we said we'd both play for equal time. But can I just have a little more time to finish this level of the game?

_____
_____
_____
_____

Are You a Good Listener?

Name: _____

We connect with other people by talking to them. But listening is important, too! Being a good listener shows someone that you care. Think about what makes a good listener.

Take this survey to see how good your listening skills are. For each item, write an **X** to rate yourself as follows:

> 1-never   2-sometimes   3-usually   4-always

	1	2	3	4
1. I look at the person who is talking.				
2. I think about what the person is saying.				
3. I only think about what I want to say next.				
4. I interrupt the person.				
5. I ask questions to make sure I understand the person.				

Would you like to be a better listener? _____

Be mindful the next time you talk to someone.

Social and Emotional Learning Activities • EMC 6097 • © Evan-Moor Corp.

Friends Can Disagree

Name: _____

People don't always agree on things, and that's okay. It's important to disagree in a respectful way. Otherwise, a disagreement can turn into an argument or a fight.

Read what each person says. The person is saying something disrespectful. Rewrite what the person said in a more respectful way.

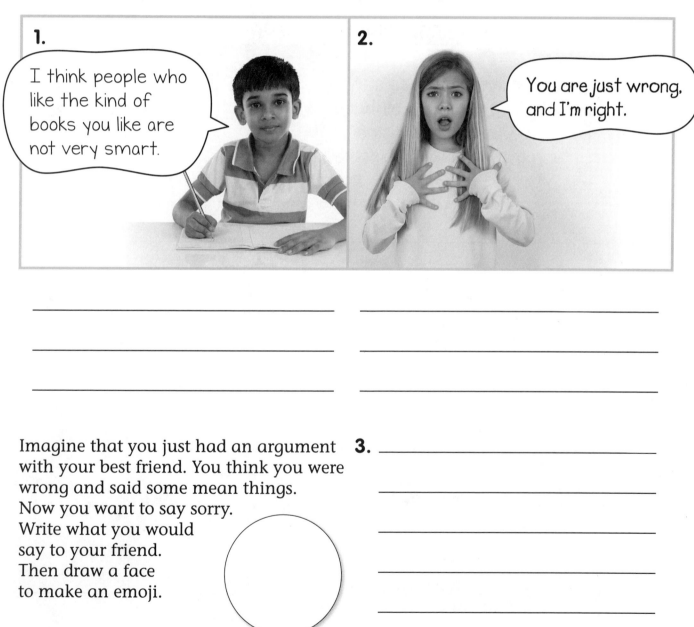

1.

I think people who like the kind of books you like are not very smart.

2.

You are just wrong, and I'm right.

_____   _____

_____   _____

_____   _____

Imagine that you just had an argument with your best friend. You think you were wrong and said some mean things. Now you want to say sorry. Write what you would say to your friend. Then draw a face to make an emoji.

3. _____

_____

_____

_____

_____

Awkward Situations

Sometimes a situation is awkward, or uncomfortable. For example, having to say sorry can be awkward sometimes. Everybody has to deal with awkward situations.

Read the story. Rate how awkward this situation would be for you by circling the number of "awkward" emojis. Then write to explain your rating.

(1 = not awkward   5 = very awkward)

1.   You got a text from someone in your class. He is inviting you to his birthday party. He is nice. But the party is at a rock-climbing gym, and you are scared of heights.

_____

_____

2.   You borrowed a book from your friend. She asked you to bring it to school and return it to her. Every day, you plan to bring the book to school, but you keep forgetting.

_____

_____

3.   Your friend forgot his homework. Now he wants you to show him your homework so he can copy it.

_____

_____

Different Cultures

People from different cultures and families sometimes have different beliefs and different ways of doing things. Everyone can learn from other people. Everyone's culture and customs should be respected.

Look at the picture and read the description. Then answer the question.

1. Pretend you have different family customs from Julia, and she told you about her family's mealtime traditions. What would be the more respectful thing to say to Julia?

   ○ That's so lame. I would hate it if my family made me try foods from other countries.

   ○ We do not do that in my family, but it sounds good.

   Julia's family tries the cuisine of a different country every Friday. Her family eats dinner together every night.

2. Pretend you have a different culture from Amrit, and he told you about his custom of not giving gifts with the left hand. What would be the more respectful thing to say to Amrit?

   ○ That is such an interesting custom. I have never heard of that.

   ○ That makes no sense to me at all. Indian culture is weird.

   Amrit's family is from India. His grandma and mom told him that they believe it is bad luck to give a gift using the left hand.

What Do You Mean?

Sometimes you can tell how people feel or what they think by looking at their face or body. When a person's face or body gives clues about how he or she feels, it's called **body language**.

The pictures show people using body language to communicate. Write what you think they are trying to say.

1.

_____

2.

_____

3.

_____

4.

_____

All About My Friend

Name: _____

Draw and write.

This is a picture of me and my friend doing something we like to do:

1.

2. My friend's name:

3. My friend's age:

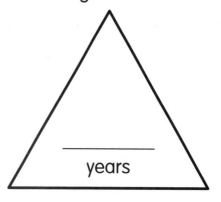

_____
years

4. One thing we do for fun:

5. One thing my friend likes to eat:

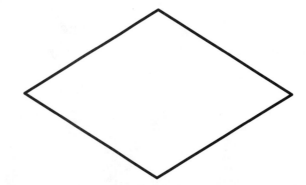

Compliments

A **compliment** is something nice that you can say to someone when you like something about that person. Sometimes a compliment can make a person's day a little bit better.

Read the compliment in the speech bubble. Then write a response to the compliment. You can choose one from the boxes below or write your own.

I'm glad you liked it.

Thank you so much!

Oh! You made my day!

Thanks for telling me.

I liked the story you wrote. It made me laugh.

Inside the star, write a compliment that you wish someone would give to you.

A Good Friend

Name: _____

Anybody can be a good friend. Friends are people we feel like we belong with, kind of like family. What makes a good friend?

Solve the puzzle about being a good friend. Read the clues to figure out the words. Write the words in the puzzle.

Crossword puzzle:
- 1 Across / 1 Down: **I** _ V _ | 2 **T** _
- 3 Down: **H**
- 4: _ _ _ | **E**
- **K**
- 5 / 6 **L** _ **Y**
- 7 **S**
- 8 **S** _ _
- 9 _ **R** _ **E** _

Down

2. You listen to me when I _____.

3. If you fall, I will _____ you.

6. When you talk, I _____.

7. If you forget your lunch, I will _____ mine.

Across

1. I will _____ you to my party.

4. We _____ the same things.

5. We can _____ together.

8. If you are _____, I will comfort you.

9. You are my _____.

Same and Different

Name: _____ • EMC 6097 • © Evan-Moor Corp.

Friends don't have to like all the same things. We can be the same in some ways and different in other ways. We can still be friends!

In the Venn diagram, write two things that you like that your friend doesn't. Write two things your friend likes that you don't. And in the middle, write two things that you both like.

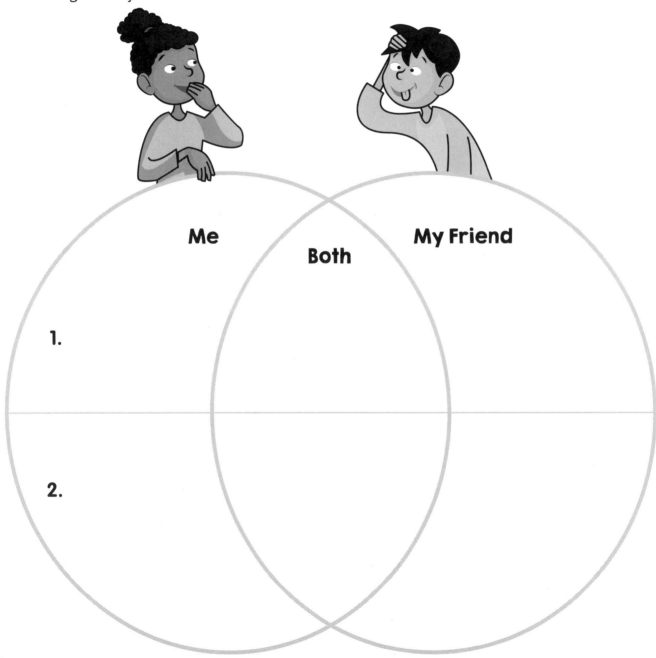

Me

Both

My Friend

1.

2.

Social and Emotional Learning Activities • EMC 6097 • © Evan-Moor Corp.

SEL and Writing

Introduce SEL and writing to your students.

One way that we can let others know how we feel is to write our feelings. We can write an email or a letter. We can make a card. Or we can write a short message. Writing to communicate can be very different from speaking. When you speak, there is usually someone else who is talking to you. But with writing, you can take your time and choose your words carefully. You can write down everything you want to say without anyone interrupting. Some people like to communicate through writing. But writing is not just for telling others how you feel or what you think. You can choose to write in a journal that only you will read. You can choose to write your own stories. You can write your own jokes. You can write your own songs or poems. Or you can just write and write and write, and it doesn't even have to make sense! When you write, you are free to write whatever you want. There are no rules or limits to what you can write. So write about anything at all, as long as you keep writing!

Topics covered in this unit:

Optimism	Gratitude	Fear
Point of view	Recognition	Emotions
Opinions	Choices	

Will It Be Okay?

Sometimes it's not possible to be cheerful and happy, and that's okay. When you feel like things are not so great, see if you can find anything good or anything that is not so bad about the situation. If you can't find anything good, that is okay. But if you try, you just might find something.

Read about Enrique's situation. Then read what he thinks is **okay** about it and what is **not so great**.

Situation	It's okay	Not so great
Enrique's teacher said there would be a social studies quiz the next day.	I am going to study and do my best on that quiz tomorrow!	I don't have enough time to study. There is no way I'll do well on that quiz.

Read the situations below. Then write one thing that could be okay and one thing that could be not so great.

Situation	It's okay	Not so great
Your parents ordered you a new video game online. But the wrong thing was delivered, and your game didn't arrive.		
You asked your mom to buy strawberries when she went shopping, but she forgot to buy them.		

Do You Want to Be a Slug?

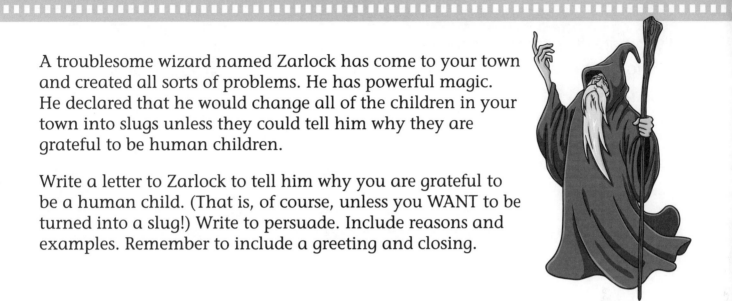

A troublesome wizard named Zarlock has come to your town and created all sorts of problems. He has powerful magic. He declared that he would change all of the children in your town into slugs unless they could tell him why they are grateful to be human children.

Write a letter to Zarlock to tell him why you are grateful to be a human child. (That is, of course, unless you WANT to be turned into a slug!) Write to persuade. Include reasons and examples. Remember to include a greeting and closing.

Date: _____

_____

_____

_____

_____

_____

_____

_____

_____ ,

_____

Send Your Fears Packing!

Everybody has fears. Because we all feel afraid sometimes, it is important not to blame or make fun of other people for their fears. Being afraid is just part of being a person.

Pretend you want to pack away all your fears. Think about the things that scare you. Write a list of all the things in the suitcase.

Choose your biggest fear from the list you wrote. Write one reason why this is something you are afraid of.

_____

_____

See Both Sides

Have you ever heard the idea that "there are two sides to every story"? It means that every person sees things a little bit differently. Everyone's point of view matters, including your own.

Mitra and Dylan are friends, but last Friday they were mad at each other. Mitra invited a bunch of their friends to go to the Ninja Gym on Saturday. Her parents own the gym. Dylan was mad that he wasn't invited. He walked over to her on his crutches and said, "The Ninja Gym is lame. I didn't want to go anyway!" Mitra got mad. Now they don't play together at recess anymore, and they try not to talk to each other.

Read Mitra's and Dylan's sides to the story. Write an **X** in the white box if you agree with or understand the point of view, even if you only kind of agree.

Mitra's side:

"I didn't invite Dylan because I thought he would be bored at the gym. He broke his leg, and I knew he wouldn't be able to jump on the trampolines and do the other activities that I wanted to do with my friends. I'm mad because he said mean things about the gym! It's not lame."

Dylan's side:

"My feelings are hurt that Mitra didn't invite me to the gym. I don't really think the gym is lame, but I wanted to hurt Mitra's feelings because she hurt my feelings first. Even though my leg is broken, I could have watched our friends play. I could have decided for myself if I wanted to go or not."

Write about a time that you had a point of view or belief different from someone else. Did it cause an argument? Did you talk to the other person and hear that person's point of view? Tell about what happened, and write details.

_____

_____

_____

_____

_____

_____

The chart shows statements that are **not great to say** and statements that are **okay to say** when you have a different opinion from another person. Finish the chart. Write your own statement under each section.

Not great to say	Okay to say
You don't know what you're talking about.	I want to know why you have that opinion. Please explain it to me.
My opinion is more important than yours.	We can figure this out if we hear each other out.
_____ _____ _____	_____ _____ _____

TV Shout-out!

Name: _____

A shout-out is a short public message that gives someone credit or attention for something good. People usually give shout-outs to those they care about.

Imagine that you won a raffle. The prize? A famous TV show host will say a special shout-out that you wrote! She will say it on live television, and millions of people in your country will hear it.

Read the example shout-out below. Then write your own shout-outs for someone in the starbursts on page 74. Last, cut them out and give them to the people you wrote them for.

Example shout-out:

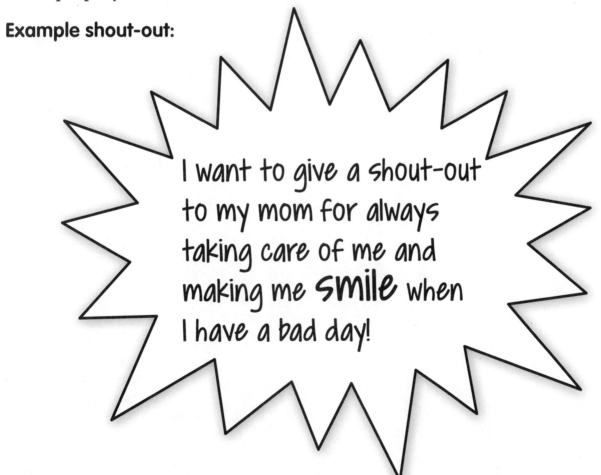

I want to give a shout-out to my mom for always taking care of me and making me smile when I have a bad day!

Shout-out for one of your friends!

Shout-out for a family member!

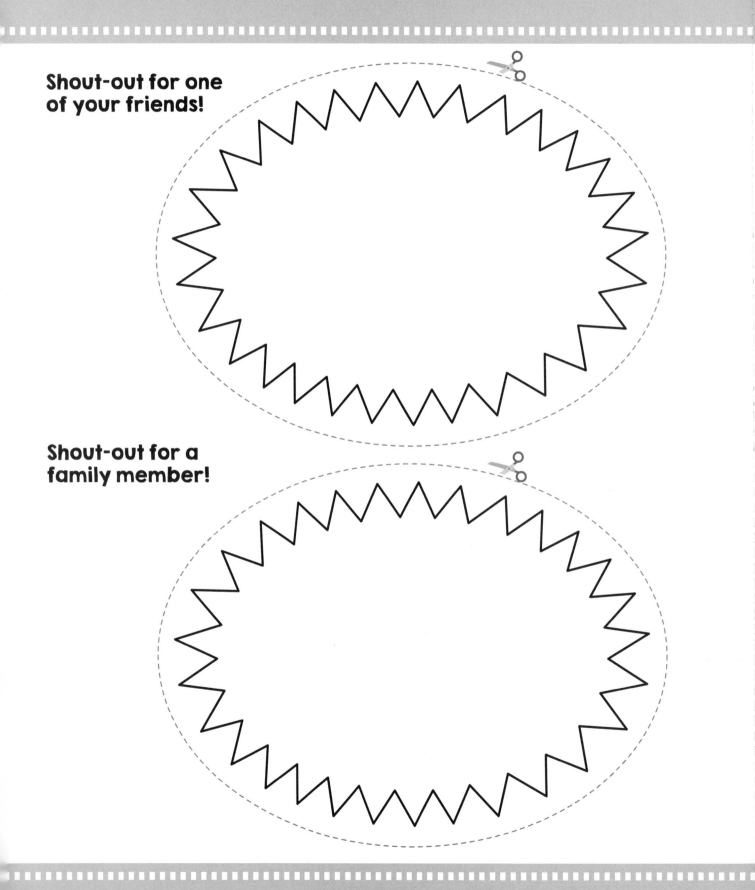

Rain, Rain

Name: _____

Some people like when it rains. They like the sound of the rain on the roof, and it makes them feel cozy. Some people don't like when it rains. The dark clouds make them think of sad things. Everyone has different feelings about different things.

Write a sentence that tells how you feel when it rains. Then write two reasons why you feel that way.

1. _____

_____

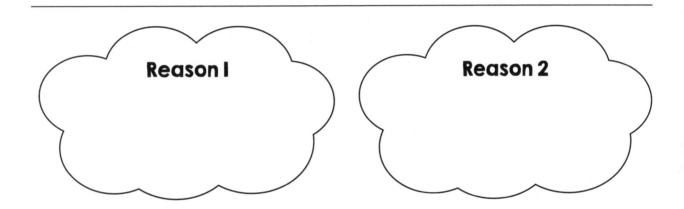

Reason 1

Reason 2

Read each sentence below. Then write an **X** in the cloud under **True** or **False** to tell if the sentence is true for you.

True   **False**

2. Sometimes I feel angry when someone says they have a different opinion from me about something.

3. I think all my friends should feel the same way that I do about things.

4. I think it is a good thing that every person has different feelings and opinions about things.

Yes-No List

Making choices is not always easy. Some people find it helpful to make a yes-no list to help them choose.

Write something that you are trying to decide. Write one of your choices in each circle. Then write one reason you might say **YES** and one reason you might say **NO** for each choice.

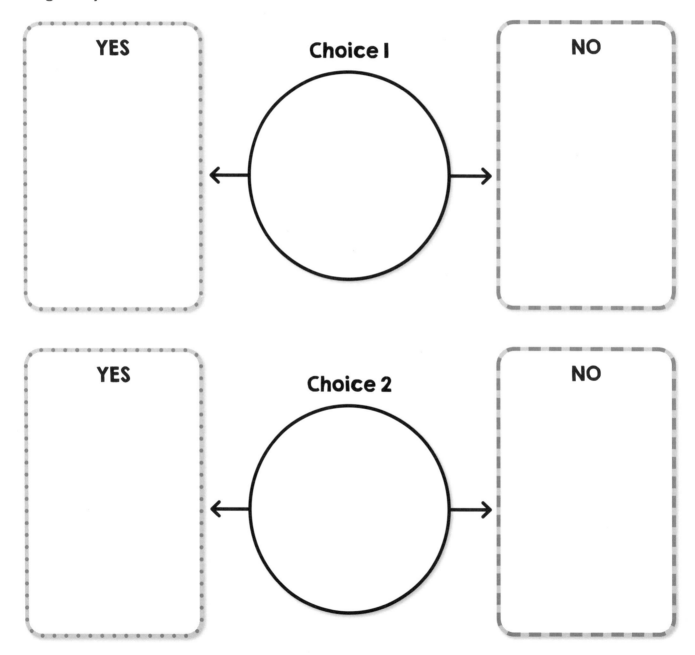

YES

Choice 1

NO

YES

Choice 2

NO

SEL and Reading

Introduce SEL and reading to your students.

When you read, you get to learn about a character's experience, or what a character is going through. Fictional characters often have the same problems that people have in real life. That's why we can learn from both fiction and nonfiction stories. We can learn how characters deal with problems and how their choices affect others. We can learn about the kinds of feelings that characters or real people have. Reading can also help us learn about different cultures, different families, and life in different places. We can imagine the characters' lives and think about how our own lives are different and the same. Trying to understand how a character feels helps some people to better understand how people in the real world feel. When you read, think about the story and see if you can take away a message or lesson that can help you in your life.

Topics covered in this unit:

Mindfulness	Choices and consequences	Tact
Respect	Empathy	Conflict resolution
Self-esteem	Acceptance	Listening skills

The Inner Beasties

Read the story. Then answer the items on page 80.

Dad's weather app said it was the hottest day of the year. Mom and Dad usually controlled how hot or cold the house was with the air system, but it was broken. So Dad went to the store to buy a fan. But the store was all sold out! When he came home empty-handed, Jayden and Ciara groaned loudly. Ciara wouldn't stop complaining.

"Hey," Dad said with a chuckle, "don't blame me for the weather!"

The kids tried playing outside, but Ciara came back in after five minutes. And two minutes later, Jayden followed. "I'm so sweaty," he thought as he headed to the freezer. He reached for a popsicle, but there were none left. Jayden gritted his teeth as he opened the fridge to see if there was any more lemonade. There wasn't.

Then he heard Ciara slurping loudly in the next room. "Ciara! Ciara!" Jayden yelled. Ciara didn't reply, so Jayden stomped over to her. "Ciara, really? You finished the popsicles and the cold lemonade. You're so selfish!"

"Don't yell at me!" Ciara yelled back with tears in her eyes.

Suddenly, the children heard the quiet, gentle voice of their mother, who had been standing in the hallway listening the entire time. "Oh, gosh," she said, "I think all of our inner beasties are coming out because we're all a bit uncomfortable."

Jayden wrinkled his nose. "What's an inner beastie?" he asked.

Social and Emotional Learning Activities • EMC 6097 • © Evan-Moor Corp.

"It's the teeny, tiny monster that lives inside all of us," Mom said with a shrug. "It only tries to come out when we are not feeling so great. You see, usually, you're just Jayden, and Ciara is just Ciara. And Jayden and Ciara are respectful, kind, and thoughtful. But we all have an inner beastie that tries to come out sometimes."

"That's scary," said Ciara.

"Well, you don't have to be afraid of your inner beastie," said Mom, "because your inner beastie is just letting you know that something isn't quite right. Sometimes my inner beastie comes out when I am too hungry. Then I know I need to eat. Sometimes my inner beastie comes out when I am sleepy. Then I know I need to rest." Jayden and Ciara listened carefully. "But you must beware," Mom continued. "If you do not try to take some time to feel better and figure out why you're not feeling so great, your inner beastie will not go away. In fact, the beastie will get bigger, and bigger, and BIGGER! And you don't want that to happen, because then the inner beastie will just take over everything you do! And instead of being Ciara and Jayden, you'll be little beasties!"

Ciara and Jayden shivered even though it was still hot. "I better get control of my inner beastie and get her to calm down right away," Ciara said. "I'm going to squeeze some lemons and make a new jug of lemonade for Jayden and the whole family right now!" As she sped out of the room, Mom winked at Jayden, and he smiled. And there were no more beasties yelling that day!

The Inner Beasties Activity

Name: _____

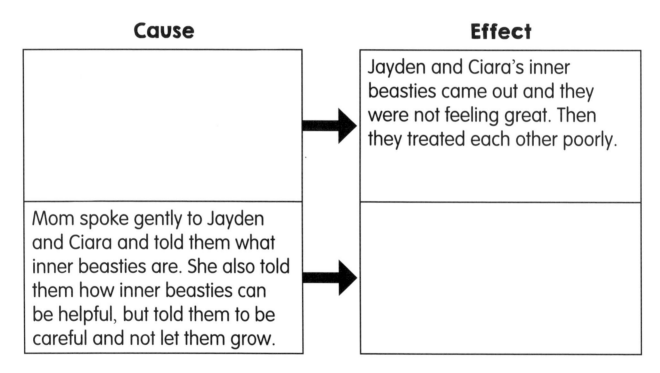

Answer the items about the story you read.

1. How are the inner beasties like people's feelings?

_____

_____

2. Think about the story. Then finish the chart. Write a cause and an effect from the story.

Cause		Effect
	→	Jayden and Ciara's inner beasties came out and they were not feeling great. Then they treated each other poorly.
Mom spoke gently to Jayden and Ciara and told them what inner beasties are. She also told them how inner beasties can be helpful, but told them to be careful and not let them grow.	→	

3. Write one thing that brings out your inner beastie.

_____

_____

Words Can Affect People

Name: _____

Read what Nebiyat said to her friend Eduardo. Then draw a line to match it to what is likely to happen.

1. Nebiyat said, "Why would I want to come to your house? My house is more fun."

2. Nebiyat asked, "Why do you always bring weird smelly food for lunch?"

Eduardo will have hurt feelings.

Eduardo will gladly invite Nebiyat to his house again in the future.

Eduardo might feel like he has to change his food choices to fit in with others.

Eduardo will feel like other people accept him for who he is.

Read what Khloe said to her friend Abdul. Then draw a line to the response from Abdul that shows empathy, or that shows that Abdul is trying to understand how Khloe feels.

3. Khloe said, "My mom is upset with me because I watched TV after school yesterday, and I forgot to get my homework done."

Abdul said, "Sometimes it's hard to get everything done that we need to do."

Abdul said, "It sounds like it's your fault that she's upset with you."

The School Play

Name: _____

We all have problems. Sometimes we try to ignore them. Sometimes they make us feel angry. But it's important that we deal with our problems in a healthy and respectful way.

Read the story.

Mr. A's class was going to put on a play. The play was Giang's idea. He loved to write. He planned out everything that would happen in the play. But Sasha thought the main character needed a friend. Roberto said Giang should add a chase scene. And Melody wanted to include a dance. Giang felt like they were ganging up on him because they wanted to change everything. "I don't like any of those ideas!" he said. "I already wrote the play, and I'm not changing it."

Rosa wanted to play the lead role in the play. Then she remembered that Jen had been in lots of plays before. When Mr. A asked who wanted to play the lead, Jen raised her hand. Rosa didn't, but she felt miserable. She thought, "Could I act as well as Jen?"

Fill in the chart for each character.

Giang

Problem	How it was handled	A better way to handle it

Rosa

Problem	How it was handled	A better way to handle it

Social and Emotional Learning Activities • EMC 6097 • © Evan-Moor Corp.

Meeting New People

Read the story. Then answer the items on page 84.

Jake was nervous. This was his first time flying on a plane. But he was even more nervous about the family reunion. He and his parents were flying to Wyoming, and he was going to meet cousins, aunts, and uncles whom he'd never met before. Were they going to like him?

Jake put on his earbuds so he could listen to music. The music made him feel less nervous. Soon the flight was over, and they were driving to his uncle's house.

As they parked, Jake could see his cousin Julian playing with some other kids on the lawn. Jake already knew Julian, but not the other kids.

When he got out of the car, it felt like a blur. A lot of people came rushing up to Jake and his parents. Lots of people were talking. "This is your cousin Marvin," one person said. "Oh, is this Jake?" another person said. "Jake, you're so big!" someone hollered. "You're my nephew, Jake," another person said. Suddenly, an older girl grabbed Jake's hand and led him to where all the other kids were.

"I'm your cousin Madison," the older girl said, smiling.

"Whoa, you're my cousin?" Jake asked with a smile. He was surprised, because she looked very different from him. Even her accent was different from his. Jake liked how she was wearing a track suit, just like him.

"Of course, silly!" she replied, laughing. "I'm your cousin, and so are my three brothers and my two sisters. We're going to have so much fun!"

83

Meeting New People,
continued

Name: _____

Answer the items as you think about the story you read.

1. Write 4 things that you have felt nervous about.

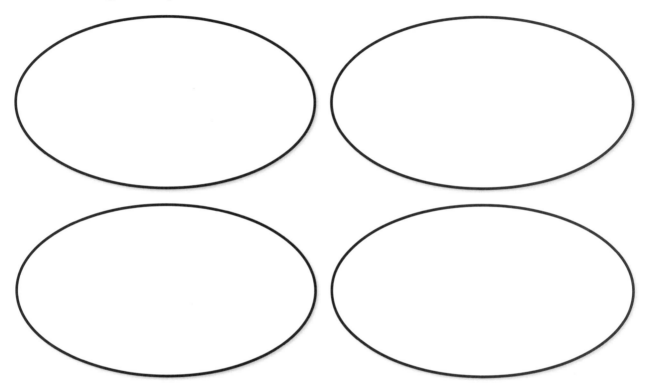

2. Have you ever been surprised by how someone else looked when you first met him or her? Fill in the circle. ○ yes   ○ no

Explain why you chose the answer you did.

_____

_____

_____

_____

Listen Bot 3000

A big part of being a good friend is being a good listener. When you're a good listener, you pay attention to the person who is speaking. You show the person that you care about what they have to say.

Read the story. It takes place in the future.

It was the first day of school at Delmar Elementary School. The year was 3021, and everybody wore helmets with face screens in front. The face screens were like little televisions. To move the face screen, all you had to do was press a button on the helmet. And that's exactly what Manuel did when he saw his friend Thalia in the hallway. He was excited to tell her about his trip to the moon. He pressed a button to move his face screen out of the way.

"My family spent three weeks there," he said. "We visited Crater Park, and…"

"Uh-huh," Thalia said. But she wasn't really listening. She was watching a video on her own face screen.

Professor Zapp was in the hallway, too, and he saw how sad Manuel looked when Thalia didn't listen to him. He noticed this happening a lot lately. Instead of listening to their friends, students were busy with their own face screens. Professor Zapp shook his head. "I must solve this problem!"

Explain the problem with the face screens.

_____

_____

_____

Name: _____

Read more of the story below.

    Professor Zapp worked all night. Finally, he smiled.
"This will solve the problem!"

    Manuel came to school the next day feeling down.
"Hello." A robot rolled over. "I am Listen Bot 3000."
Manuel scratched his head. "What do you do?"
"I listen," Listen Bot 3000 said. "Would you like to tell me something?"
Manuel shrugged. Then he told Listen Bot 3000 about his moon trip.
Listen Bot 3000 nodded. "Wow. That is amazing. I'm glad you had fun."
Manuel felt happier after talking to Listen Bot 3000.

Is Listen Bot 3000 a good solution to the problem? Make a list of PROS and CONS. Write 2 in each column.

PROS	CONS
1.	
2.	

SEL and Math

Introduce SEL and math to your students.

Some people like doing math, and some people don't. It's okay to like or not like math. Even if you don't like it, math is still an important skill. Some people don't like math because they think they are not good at it. No person is good at everything, and it is okay to make mistakes. Just remember that you can improve at anything if you keep trying and keep practicing. And if you keep trying to do math, you might even find that you actually like it!

Topics covered in this unit:

Different approaches	Mistakes	Grit
Mindfulness	Goals	Emotions
Social cues	Manners	

Different Ways
I Can Solve It!

Name: _____

When a problem is difficult, remember that it DOES have a solution. And you can find the solution if you keep trying. You might find it helpful to try different ways of solving it and see which way you like best.

Read how all three students like to solve math problems.

Jamie likes to draw pictures.

Troy likes to multiply.

Ines likes to use addition.

Show how each student would solve the math problem in the box below.

There are 2 classes. Each class has 28 students. The classes are having a picnic together. The teachers will eat salads, and the students will eat hot dogs. Each student can have 2 hot dogs. How many hot dogs do the teachers need to buy?

1. How would Jamie solve it?

2. How would Troy solve it?

3. How would Ines solve it?

Made a Mistake?
It's Okay, Fix It!

Name: _____

When you are trying to solve a math problem, it is okay to make mistakes. The great thing about math is that if you make a mistake, you can try to solve the problem again.

You are helping your friend with math homework. Read the problem. Look at the work your friend showed, as well as the answer. Then answer the questions.

1.

Problem	Work Shown	Answer
Taneesha has 15 comic books. Carlos has double that. Julie has 3 fewer comic books than Taneesha. How many comic books do the three friends have in all?	$\begin{array}{r} \overset{1}{15} \\ \times\ 3 \\ \hline 45 \end{array}$ $\begin{array}{r} \overset{1}{15} \\ 45 \\ +12 \\ \hline 72 \end{array}$ $15 - 3 = 12$	They have 72 comic books in all.

Is your friend's answer correct?   ○ yes   ○ no

Why or why not? _____

_____

Look at each solved math problem in the circle. If it is correct, write **correct** in the connecting circle. If the solution is incorrect, write an **X** to cross out the wrong answer, and write the correct answer in the connecting circle.

2. (59 + 17 = 68)——( )

3. (36 – 17 = 19)——( )

Thinking About My Learning!

Name: _____

Just like a sponge takes in water and grows, your brain takes in information and grows when you learn new things. Stop and think about what you know in math today that you didn't know last year. You may be surprised at just how much you've learned!

Use numbers, words, or pictures to answer each question.

What are three things you know in math now that you didn't know last year?

What are three things you can't do in math now that you hope to learn?

Symmetrical Feeling Faces

Name: _____

Sometimes you can tell how someone is feeling by looking at his or her face. Look at the mouth, the eyes, the eyebrows, and the forehead.

Look at each half of a face. Then draw the other half to match. Look carefully at the face and figure out what feeling it shows. Write it below.

1.

_____

2.

_____

3.

_____

4.

_____

Learning from Problems

Having a problem in your life can be no fun. It's okay to not be happy about a problem. If you can, try to think of problems as things that can help you learn. Sometimes we can learn from problems and mistakes.

Solve the math problems. Then find each answer below the line with the matching number. The letters will spell out a message about learning from our problems.

A	E	G	I	L
567	939	116	642	324
− 421	− 774	+ 115	− 333	+ 125

N	O	R	S	W
418	212	918	266	855
+ 269	+ 486	− 216	+ 542	+ 103

L ___ ___ ___ ___ ___ ___ ___
449 165 146 702 687 309 687 231

___ ___   ___ ___ ___ ___ ___ ___ ___
309 808   231 702 698 958 309 687 231

What Should I Say?

If you pay too much at a store, you need to get change back. **Change** is the difference between what was owed and what was paid. If you do not get the correct amount of change back, use respectful language to say it.

Read what happened at a yard sale. Then answer the items.

Leslie bought three books at a yard sale. The books cost 1 dollar, 3 dollars, and 7 dollars. Leslie paid 20 dollars. The seller gave her 10 dollars in change.

1. How much did Leslie owe for the books? _____ dollars

2. How much should the seller have given Leslie in change? _____ dollars

3. Write what Leslie could say in a respectful way to let the seller know about the mistake.

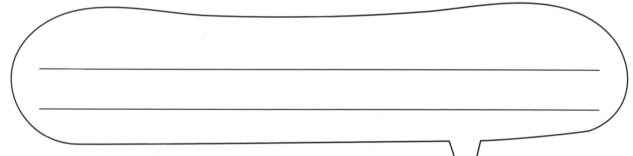
_____
_____

4. Color the circles next to the things that Leslie should NOT say if she is being respectful.

○ Don't you know how to count?

○ Thank you, but can we count the change again?

○ Sorry, but this change is incorrect.

○ Give me the correct change right now!

Manners Graph

Name: _____ • EMC 6097 • © Evan-Moor.

When we use manners, it shows that we care about other people's comfort. Some manners are different around the world. What manners do you use?

Write a number to finish each sentence. It is okay to guess.

Thank you!

1. I've said "please" or "thank you" _____ times this week.

2. I've waited for my turn _____ times this week.

Finish the sentence to tell about another manner you used this week and how many times.

3. I've _____ times
this week.

Color the graph to show how many times you've used these manners.

4.

	Said "please" or "thank you"	Waited my turn	Other
10			
9			
8			
7			
6			
5			
4			
3			
2			
1			

Social and Emotional Learning Activities • EMC 6097 • © Evan-Moor Corp.

Pinwheel Breathing

Watching patterns move can help some people feel cozy and relaxed. Some people also feel relaxed when they breathe in and out slowly.

You will make a pinwheel with a pattern. Then you can watch the pattern move as you breathe in and out slowly.

What You Need

- pinwheel pattern on page 96
- crayons or markers
- a pencil with an eraser on the end

- scissors
- a tack or a pin

What You Do

1. Cut out the pinwheel shape on page 96. Then cut along the dotted lines.

2. Draw and color shapes to make a pattern on both sides of the pinwheel.

3. Find the dot in one of the corners of the pinwheel. Pull that corner toward the center dot. Hold it in place with one finger. Don't make a fold or crease.

4. Repeat with the other three corners, holding them all in place in the center.

5. Hold the pencil behind the pinwheel, with the eraser touching the pinwheel at the center. Stick the tack or pin through all four corners and into the eraser.

6. Use the pinwheel. Breathe in slowly, counting to 4 in your head. When you breathe out, gently blow on the pinwheel. The pinwheel will spin while you blow on it. Notice how the shape pattern changes as it spins. Repeat, breathing in and out slowly, counting and blowing on the pinwheel. Pay attention to how you feel.

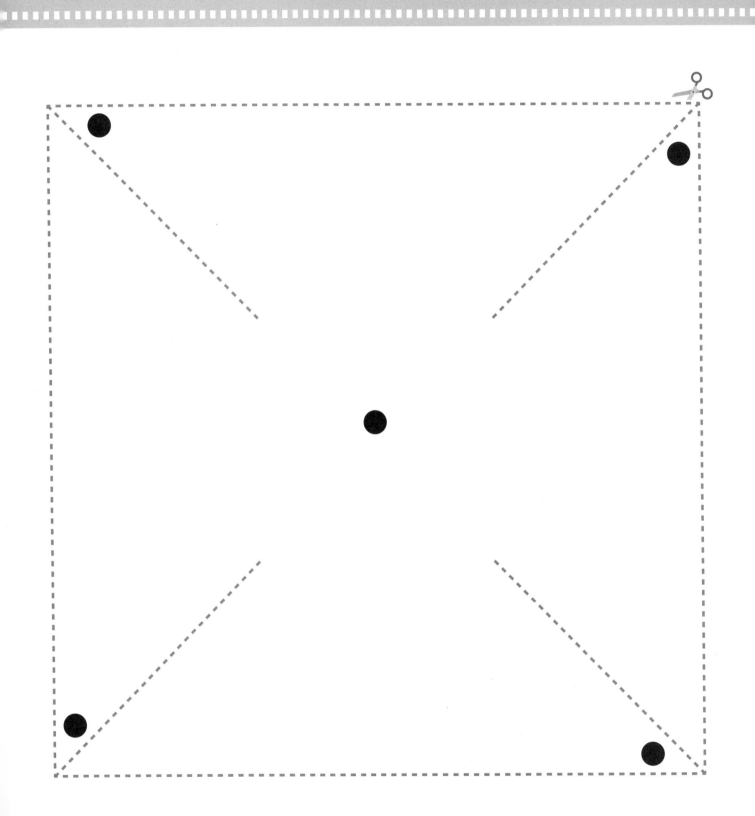

SEL and Social Studies

Introduce SEL and social studies to your students.

All people are different in a lot of ways. But all people are the same in so many ways, too. Social studies helps us learn about all kinds of people. We can learn about people who may look different from us or speak a different language. We can learn about people who live in different places or who do things differently from us. Social studies lets us learn about how people did things a long time ago. It also teaches us about the kinds of food, music, clothing, and holidays that are part of people's lives all around the world. Most importantly, social studies helps us learn about the problems that people have all around the world. We can learn about the problems people had in the past. And we can see how people come together to form a community and to work together. The more we learn about other people, the better we can understand how we are all different and the same.

Topics covered in this unit:

Rights	Point of view	Mindfulness
Cooperation	Cultural awareness	Acceptance

People's Rights

A **right** is something that all people deserve. Rights and laws are supposed to protect us and make everything fair for everyone. But not all people have had equal rights. In a fair community, all people have the same rights.

Imagine that it is the year 3000, and all of the countries in the world have come together to form one country. You are in charge of naming the country and writing a list of rights for it. Inside the diamonds, write 5 human rights that all people in the future country will have.

Bill of Rights for _____
country name

All people have the right to...

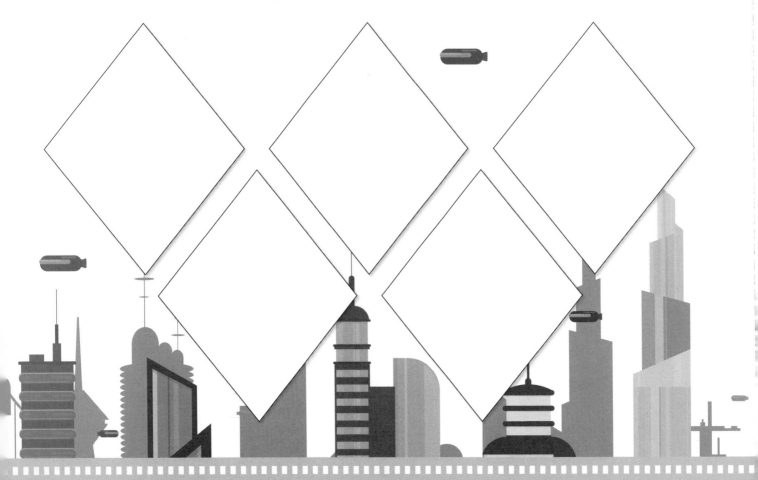

Different People, Different Lives

Name: _____

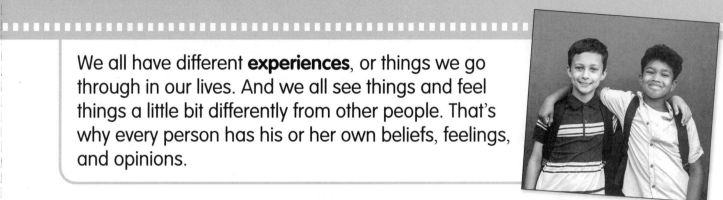

We all have different **experiences**, or things we go through in our lives. And we all see things and feel things a little bit differently from other people. That's why every person has his or her own beliefs, feelings, and opinions.

Think of your best friend. Write two things about your life that your friend does not experience. Then write things about your friend's life that you do not experience. Last, write two ways that your lives are the same.

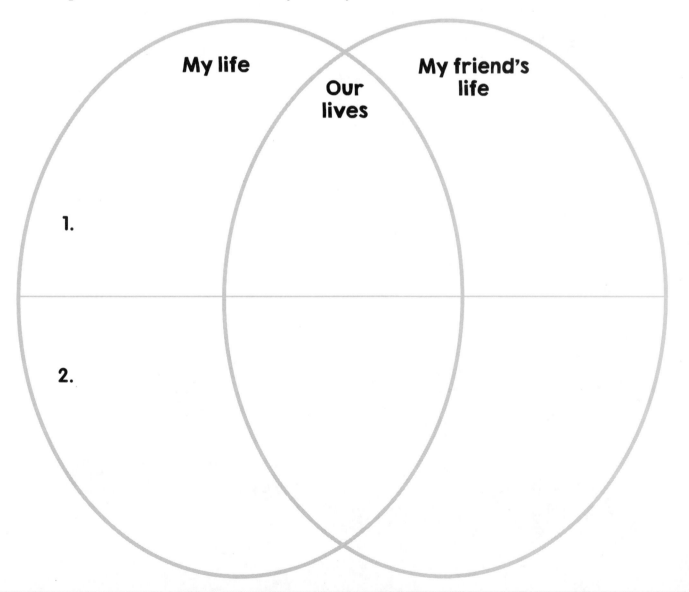

My life

Our lives

My friend's life

1.

2.

How I Feel

Name: _____

Read the words in each circle. Color the circle if the words tell how you feel or how you have felt before.

I feel like people treat me differently sometimes because of how I look.

I feel like people don't treat me as well as some other people sometimes.

I feel like my home is not as good as other people's homes.

I am not happy with the clothes or shoes I wear.

I feel like people treat me poorly sometimes because of the way I talk.

I feel like I would be happier if I were somebody else.

Social and Emotional Learning Activities • EMC 6097 • © Evan-Moor Corp.

Cooperation

Name: _____

When people **cooperate**, they work together. They listen to each other's ideas and try to help each other.

Answer the items.

Tell about a time in your own life when you chose to cooperate with others.

_____

_____

_____

Imagine that you're going to school in a country where you don't speak the language that everyone else speaks. Circle the things that will help you to cooperate with others. Draw a line through the things that will not help.

respect   shyness   a short temper   nice clothes   creativity

listening skills

effort   grit   being a bully   A LOUD VOICE

lots of money   EMPATHY

being rude   being friendly   communication skills

admitting your mistakes

My Culture

Every family has its own culture and traditions. Some families celebrate cultures from more than one country or ethnicity. In some ways, your family is different from other families. In other ways, your family is the same as other families.

Tell about your family's culture and traditions.

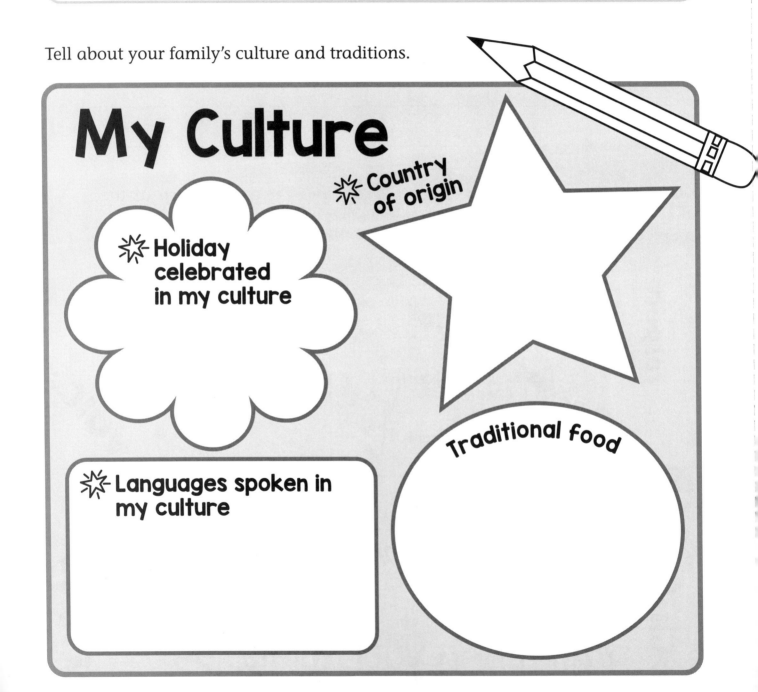

My Culture

✸ Country of origin

✸ Holiday celebrated in my culture

✸ Languages spoken in my culture

Traditional food

Is It Respectful?

Read each comment. Tell whether you think the comment is
respectful or disrespectful. Then write to explain your opinion.

1. I know you moved here from a different country,
but you need to learn how to speak our
language better. It's so hard to understand you!

_____

_____

◯ respectful
◯ disrespectful

2. I am very proud of my family's cultural background.
What makes you most proud of your family's culture?

_____

_____

◯ respectful
◯ disrespectful

3. You are very pretty for a foreign person.

_____

_____

◯ respectful
◯ disrespectful

4. I would like to learn more about your culture.

_____

_____

◯ respectful
◯ disrespectful

What's on My Plate?

Think about the foods that you and your family eat. What foods does your family eat often? Are there any foods you eat a lot because of your family's culture? Does your family like to try foods from a lot of different cultures?

Draw foods that your family eats often. Write the names of the foods, too.

Festivals at the Khatris'

Read the story. Then answer the items about the story on page 107.

Every year my best friend Jung's neighbors have celebrations in the fall and in the spring. In the fall they decorate their house with lights and lanterns inside and out. They hang decorations, they make tons of food, and they even have fireworks! In the spring, they have all their family and friends over and throw brightly colored powder into the air as they exclaim, "Have a colorful and joyous Holi!" It is amazing to see!

One fall evening Jung and I set up lawn chairs in his front yard and watched as a celebration took place next door. We didn't want to stare, but we couldn't take our eyes off of the brightly colored clothes, the rainbow of lanterns, and the groups of smiling, happy people. Our mouths were watering from the smell of spiced foods wafting through the air. There was so much excitement going on next door. Mrs. Khatri saw us sniffing the air and stretching our necks toward her front yard. We were so embarrassed, but our embarrassment turned to excitement as we pushed each other's arms, saying, "Here she comes! Shh... I bet she's going to invite us over!" We sat up as she walked toward us.

Sure enough, Mrs. Khatri said, "Hello, boys. Would you like to join our celebration?" We eagerly said yes and crossed over to her yard, heading straight for the food table.

Cauliflower Pakora

An older boy at the table could tell that we didn't know what most of the foods were. He pointed as he said, "This is Cauliflower Pakora. It's fried cauliflower. And this is Pumpkin Halwa, it's a sweet pumpkin pudding, and this is..." Before he could finish his sentence, Jung and I had already grabbed plates and were filling them up. As we sat on the Khatris' porch steps and watched the fireworks while we ate, we heard their guests say, "Happy Diwali! May every Diya you light bring you happiness and good health!" We learned that night how special a Diwali celebration is, and we haven't missed one at the Khatris' since.

When spring arrived, Jung and I saw the Khatris working in their front yard, tending to the flowers, mowing the lawn, and setting up tables. Jung and I looked at each other and said, "It must be time for the Holi festival!" We helped the Khatris set up. We smelled food cooking inside the house and knew people would be arriving soon. After Jung and I finished helping, we went back to his house to look for old t-shirts and pants to wear. We

Gulal, colorful powders

wanted to be prepared for the celebration of colors that would rain down on us. Last year when I got home, my mom and dad looked at me with the biggest smiles and said I looked like a rainbow. Jung and I had a blast being a part of the Khatris' celebrations, and we learned how much color and light bring people joy.

Name: _____

Answer the items about the story you read.

1. What two festivals do the Khatris celebrate at their home in the story?

_____

_____

2. Why do you think Mrs. Khatri decided to invite the boys to be part of the celebration?

_____

_____

3. Draw a picture of one thing from the story you want to see or experience. Then explain why you want to see or experience it.

_____

_____

_____

Cultural Differences

People from different cultures eat different foods, have different celebrations, dress differently, and speak differently. It is important to show respect for cultural differences.

Color the circles that show people respecting cultural differences.

"Eww...what's that weird smell? I think it's your lunch! Yuck!"

"I haven't seen that food before. I bet it tastes good. What is it called?"

"Why do you always wear that scarf thing on your head?"

"What language are you speaking? It sounds cool!"

"I like your hair. Is it hard to get it into that cool style?"

"Learn English! No one knows what you are saying."

Every Culture Has Art

Name: _____

People use creativity to make art. Every culture in the world has art. Art can be pictures, music, buildings, movies, statues, poems, or many other things that people may find beautiful.

Read about the work of art and look at the picture.
Then answer the question.

1. Madhubani Art is a style of Indian painting. This type of painting uses natural dyes. It is made using tools such as twigs, brushes, and matchsticks.

   Do you like this art? Why or why not?

   _____

   _____

   _____

2. This building is called Dabo Pagoda. It is also known as "the pagoda of many treasures." It is in Gyeongju, South Korea. Many people consider this to be a beautiful structure.

   Do you like this art? Why or why not?

   _____

   _____

   _____

Answer Key

Many of the activities in this book are not included in the answer key because answers vary based on each student's perspective and life experience.

Page 21

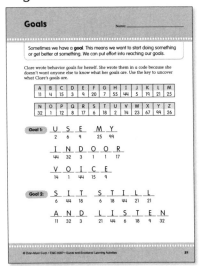

Goals

Goal 1: U S E M Y
I N D O O R
V O I C E

Goal 2: S I T S T I L L
A N D L I S T E N

Page 28

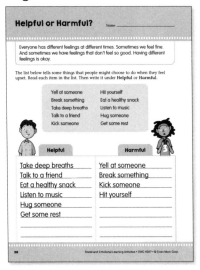

Helpful or Harmful?

Helpful
Take deep breaths
Talk to a friend
Eat a healthy snack
Listen to music
Hug someone
Get some rest

Harmful
Yell at someone
Break something
Kick someone
Hit yourself

Page 34

Feel Empathy

1. no empathy
2. empathy
3. empathy

Page 38

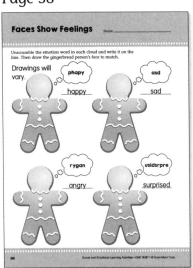

Faces Show Feelings

Drawings will vary.

phapy — happy
asd — sad
rygan — angry
usidsrpre — surprised

Page 39

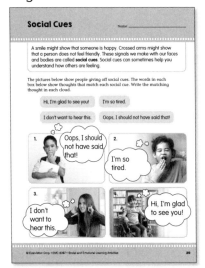

Social Cues

1. Oops, I should not have said that!
2. I'm so tired.
3. I don't want to hear this.
4. Hi, I'm glad to see you!

Page 40

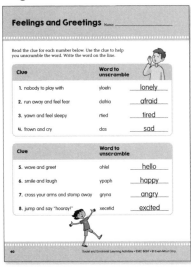

Feelings and Greetings

Clue	Word to unscramble	
1. nobody to play with	yloeln	lonely
2. run away and feel fear	dafria	afraid
3. yawn and feel sleepy	rtied	tired
4. frown and cry	das	sad

Clue	Word to unscramble	
5. wave and greet	ohlel	hello
6. smile and laugh	ypaph	happy
7. cross your arms and stomp away	gryna	angry
8. jump and say "hooray!"	xecetid	excited

Page 41

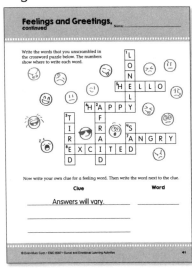

Feelings and Greetings, continued

Now write your own clue for a feeling word. Then write the word next to the clue.

Clue	Word
Answers will vary.	

Page 42

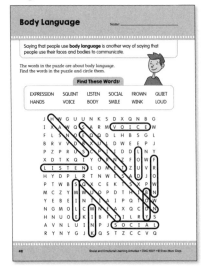

Body Language

Find These Words!
EXPRESSION SQUINT LISTEN SOCIAL FROWN QUIET
HANDS VOICE BODY SMILE WINK LOUD

Page 61

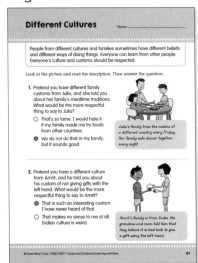

Different Cultures

1. We do not do that in my family, but it sounds good.
2. That is such an interesting custom. I have never heard of that.

Page 65

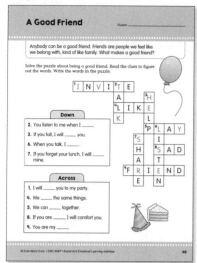

A Good Friend   Name _____

Anybody can be a good friend. Friends are people we feel like we belong with, kind of like family. What makes a good friend?

Solve the puzzle about being a good friend. Read the clues to figure out the words. Write the words in the puzzle.

Crossword answers:
¹INVITE
²ALIKE
PLAY
⁸SAD
⁹FRIEND

Down
2. You listen to me when I ____.
3. If you fall, I will ____ you.
6. When you talk, I ____.
7. If you forget your lunch, I will ____ mine.

Across
1. I will ____ you to my party.
4. We ____ the same things.
5. We can ____ together.
8. If you are ____ I will comfort you.
9. You are my ____.

Page 81

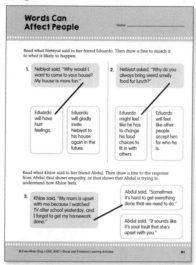

Words Can Affect People   Name _____

Read what Nebiyat said to her friend Eduardo. Then draw a line to match it to what is likely to happen.

1. Nebiyat said, "Why would I want to come to your house? My house is more fun."
   - Eduardo will have hurt feelings.
   - Eduardo will gladly invite Nebiyat to his house again in the future.

2. Nebiyat asked, "Why do you always bring weird smelly food for lunch?"
   - Eduardo might feel like he has to change his food choices to fit in with others.
   - Eduardo will feel like other people accept him for who he is.

Read what Khloe said to her friend Abdul. Then draw a line to the response from Abdul that shows empathy, or that shows that Abdul is trying to understand how Khloe feels.

3. Khloe said, "My mom is upset with me because I watched TV after school yesterday, and I forgot to get my homework done."
   - Abdul said, "Sometimes it's hard to get everything done that we need to do."
   - Abdul said, "It sounds like it's your fault that she's upset with you."

Page 88

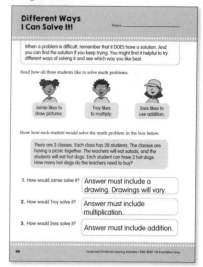

Different Ways I Can Solve It!   Name _____

When a problem is difficult, remember that it DOES have a solution. And you can find the solution if you keep trying. You might find it helpful to try different ways of solving it and see which way you like best.

Read how all three students like to solve math problems.

- Jamie likes to draw pictures.
- Troy likes to multiply.
- Ines likes to use addition.

Show how each student would solve the math problem in the box below.

There are 2 classes. Each class has 28 students. The classes are having a picnic together. The teachers will eat salads, and the students will eat hot dogs. Each student can have 2 hot dogs. How many hot dogs do the teachers need to buy?

1. How would Jamie solve it? | Answer must include a drawing. Drawings will vary.
2. How would Troy solve it? | Answer must include multiplication.
3. How would Ines solve it? | Answer must include addition.

Page 89

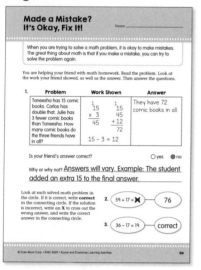

Made a Mistake? It's Okay, Fix It!   Name _____

When you are trying to solve a math problem, it is okay to make mistakes. The great thing about math is that if you make a mistake, you can try to solve the problem again.

You are helping your friend with math homework. Read the problem. Look at the work your friend showed, as well as the answer. Then answer the questions.

Problem	Work Shown	Answer
Taneesha has 15 comic books. Carlos has double that. Julie has 3 fewer comic books than Taneesha. How many comic books do the three friends have in all?	15 × 3 = 45 15 + 45 + 12 = 72 15 − 3 = 12	They have 72 comic books in all.

Is your friend's answer correct? ○ yes ● no

Why or why not? Answers will vary. Example: The student added an extra 15 to the final answer.

Look at each solved math problem in the circle. If it is correct, write **correct** in the connecting circle. If the solution is incorrect, write an X to cross out the wrong answer, and write the correct answer in the connecting circle.

2. 59 + 17 = ✘ → 76
3. 36 − 17 = 19 → correct

Page 91

Symmetrical Feeling Faces   Name _____

Sometimes you can tell how someone is feeling by looking at his or her face. Look at the mouth, the eyes, the eyebrows, and the forehead.

Look at each half of a face. Then draw the other half to match. Look carefully at the face and figure out what feeling it shows. Write it below.

1. surprised
2. happy
3. angry
4. scared

Page 92

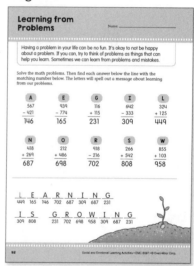

Learning from Problems   Name _____

Having a problem in your life can be no fun. It's okay to not be happy about a problem. If you can, try to think of problems as things that can help you learn. Sometimes we can learn from problems and mistakes.

Solve the math problems. Then find each answer below the line with the matching number below. The letters will spell out a message about learning from our problems.

A	E	G	I	L
567 − 421 = 146	939 − 774 = 165	116 + 115 = 231	642 − 333 = 309	324 + 125 = 449

N	O	R	S	W
418 + 269 = 687	212 + 486 = 698	918 − 216 = 702	266 + 542 = 808	855 + 103 = 958

L E A R N I N G
449 165 146 702 687 309 687 231

I S   G R O W I N G
309 808   231 702 698 958 309 687 231

Page 93

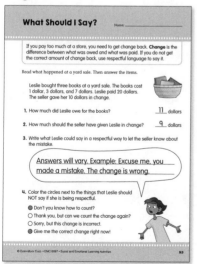

What Should I Say?   Name _____

If you pay too much at a store, you need to get change back. **Change** is the difference between what was owed and what was paid. If you do not get the correct amount of change back, use respectful language to say it.

Read what happened at a yard sale. Then answer the items.

Leslie bought three books at a yard sale. The books cost 1 dollar, 3 dollars, and 7 dollars. Leslie paid 20 dollars. The seller gave her 10 dollars in change.

1. How much did Leslie owe for the books?   11 dollars
2. How much should the seller have given Leslie in change?   9 dollars
3. Write what Leslie could say in a respectful way to let the seller know about the mistake.

   Answers will vary. Example: Excuse me, you made a mistake. The change is wrong.

4. Color the circles next to the things that Leslie should NOT say if she is being respectful.
   ● Don't you know how to count?
   ○ Thank you, but can we count the change again?
   ○ Sorry, but this change is incorrect.
   ● Give me the correct change right now!

Page 103

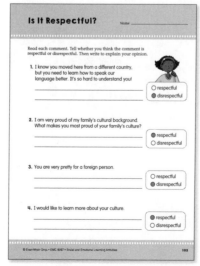

Is It Respectful?   Name _____

Read each comment. Tell whether you think the comment is respectful or disrespectful. Then write to explain your opinion.

1. I know you moved here from a different country, but you need to learn how to speak our language better. It's so hard to understand you!
   ○ respectful ● disrespectful

2. I am very proud of my family's cultural background. What makes you most proud of your family's culture?
   ● respectful ○ disrespectful

3. You are very pretty for a foreign person.
   ○ respectful ● disrespectful

4. I would like to learn more about your culture.
   ● respectful ○ disrespectful

Page 107

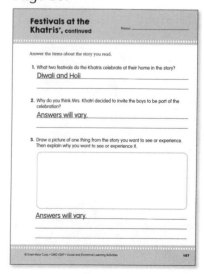

Festivals at the Khatris', continued   Name _____

Answer the items about the story you read.

1. What two festivals do the Khatris celebrate at their home in the story?
   Diwali and Holi

2. Why do you think Mrs. Khatri decided to invite the boys to be part of the celebration?
   Answers will vary.

3. Draw a picture of one thing from the story you want to see or experience. Then explain why you want to see or experience it.

   Answers will vary.

Page 108

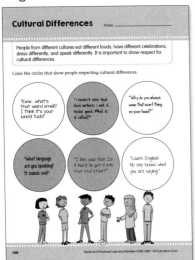

Cultural Differences

Name _____

People from different cultures eat different foods, have different celebrations, dress differently, and speak differently. It is important to show respect for cultural differences.

Color the circles that show people respecting cultural differences.

"Eww...what's that weird smell? I think it's your lunch! Yuck!"

"I haven't seen that food before. I bet it tastes good. What is it called?"

"Why do you always wear that scarf thing on your head?"

"What language are you speaking? It sounds cool!"

"I like your hair. Is it hard to get it into that cool style?"

"Learn English! No one knows what you are saying."

Social and Emotional Learning Activities • EMC 6097 • © Evan-Moor Corp.